THE USBORNE

FIRST THOUSAND WORDS IN ENGLISH

Heather Amery

Illustrated by Stephen Cartwright

Revised edition by Mairi Mackinnon

Picture editing by Mike Olley

There is a little yellow duck to look for on every double page with pictures. Can you find it?

Stephen Cartwright's little yellow duck made his first-ever appearance in *The First Thousand Words* over thirty years ago. Duck has since featured in over 125 titles, in more than 70 languages, and has delighted millions of readers, both young and old, around the world.

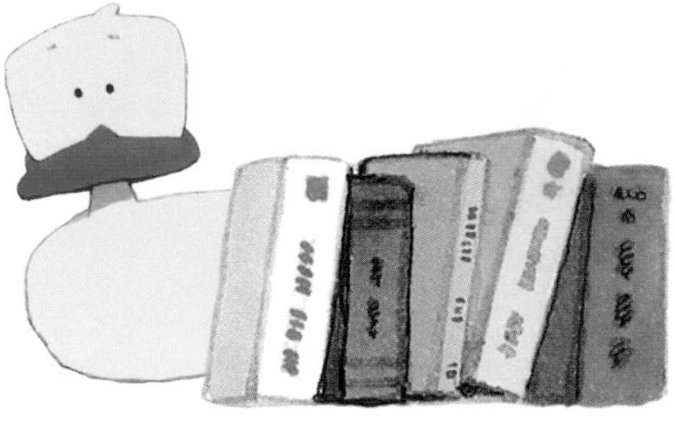

This revised edition first published in 2013 by Usborne Publishing Ltd, 83-85 Saffron Hill, London EC1N 8RT. www.usborne.com
Based on a previous title first published in 1979.

About this book

This picture word book has been designed to appeal to children at different ages, and can be used in various ways. This edition has been brought up to date to include words and objects which are common in everyday language and familiar in everyday life.

A wordbuilder for young children
For very young children, it is a bright and stimulating way of learning new words. The large pictures provide lots of opportunities for spotting and matching with the smaller pictures around the edges, and for discussing the lively scenes.

A reading and spelling guide for older children
For older children, the book can be used in the early stages of learning to read, and as a beginner's guide to spelling.

A vocabulary builder for English language learners
For children learning English as a second or additional language, it is a powerful and effective way of learning to read, say and spell new words.

Hear the words online
You can listen to all the words in the book on the Usborne website. Just go to **www.usborne.com/quicklinks** and enter the keywords **1000 english**. There you can also find links to other useful websites about the English language, Britain and the USA.

Using the wordlist
At the back of the book there is a list of all the words in alphabetical order. It can be used to encourage children to look up words and find the right page and picture. This is an important skill which will prepare children to use simple information books and dictionaries.

Remember, this is a book of a thousand words. It will take time to learn them all. This is a book to come back to again and again.

Please note that Usborne Publishing is not responsible for the content of external websites. Please follow the internet safety guidelines on the Usborne website.

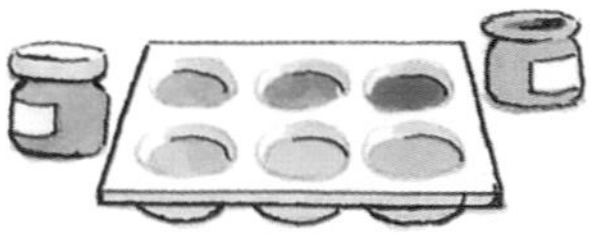
paints

bottles

goldfish

helicopter

jigsaw

chocolate

At home

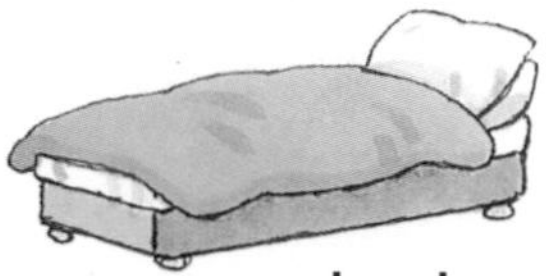

bed

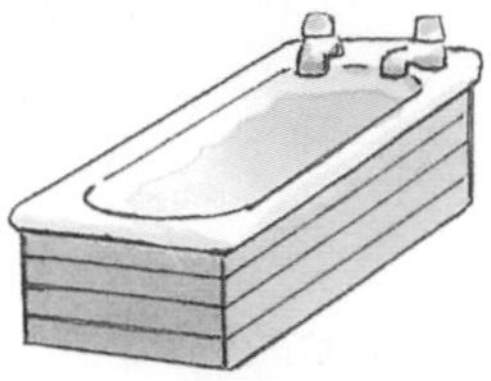

bath

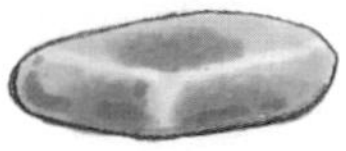

soap

tap

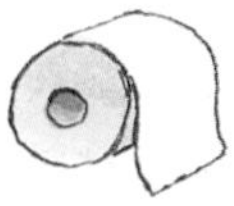

toilet paper

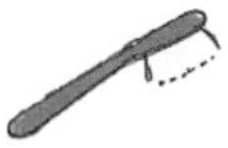

toothbrush

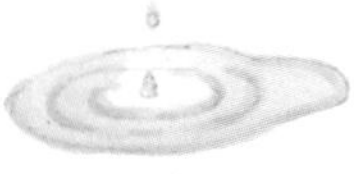

water

toilet

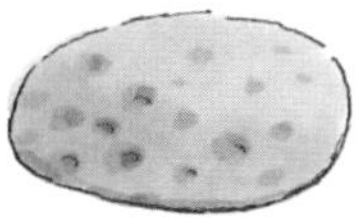

sponge

basin

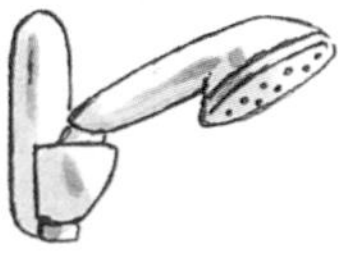

shower

bathroom

living room

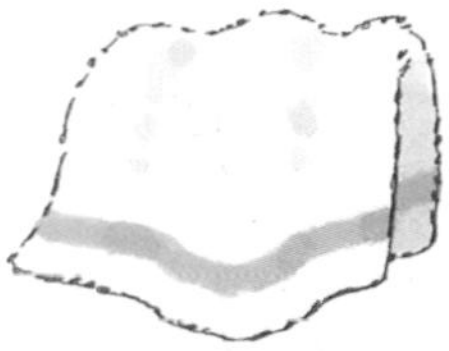

towel

toothpaste

radio

cushion

DVD

carpet

sofa

chair

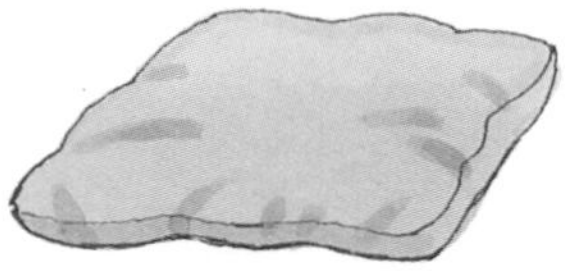
duvet

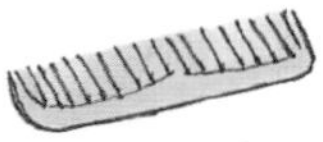
comb

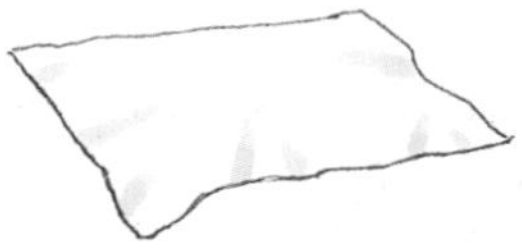
sheet

rug

wardrobe

bedroom

television

chest of drawers

mirror

brush

lamp

hall

pictures

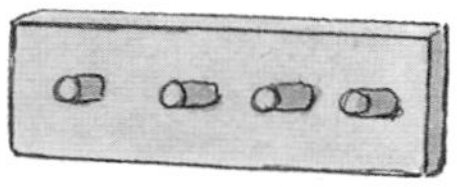
pegs

telephone

radiator

fruit

newspaper

table

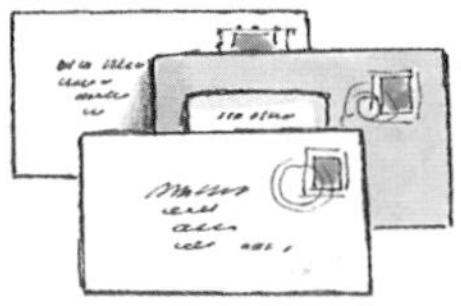
letters

stairs

The kitchen

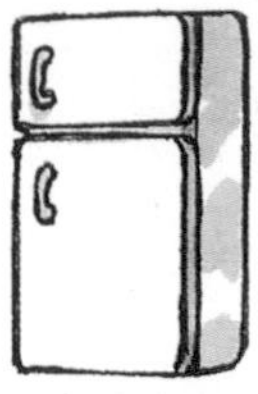
fridge

sink

glasses

clock

stool

teaspoons

switch

washing powder

key

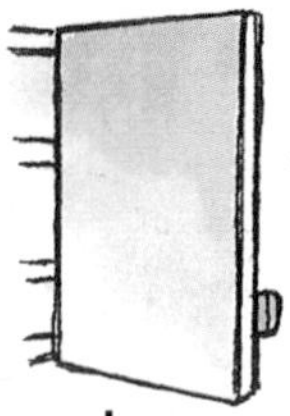
door

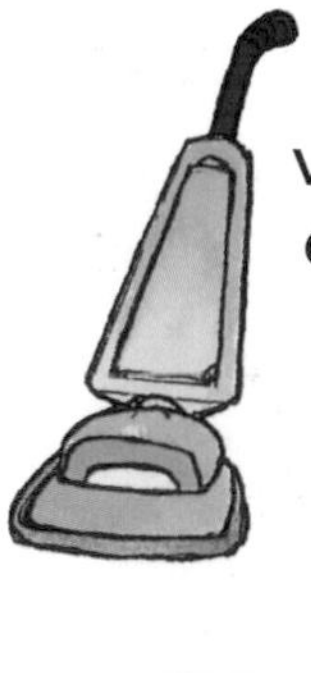
vacuum cleaner

saucepans

forks

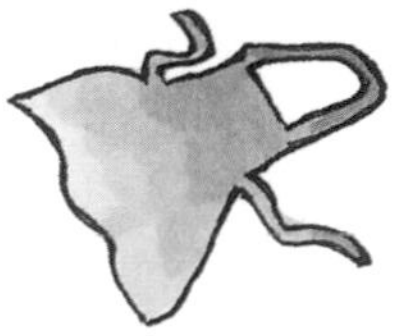
apron

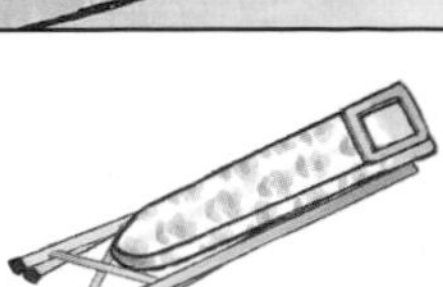
ironing board

rubbish

kettle
knives
mop
duster
tiles
broom
washing machine
dustpan
drawer
saucers
frying pan
cooker
spoons
plates
iron
tea towel
cups
matches
brush
bowls
cupboard

The garden

wheelbarrow

watering can

beehive

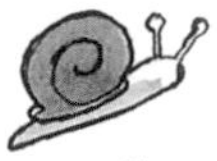

snail

bricks

pigeon

spade

ladybird

dustbin

seeds

shed

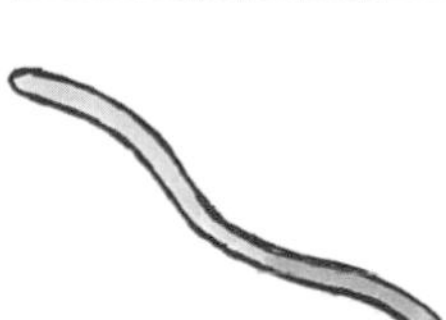

worm

flowers

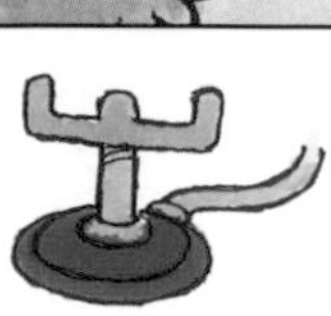

sprinkler

hoe

wasp

bee
trowel
bone
hedge
fork
lawnmower
path
leaves
tree
smoke
caterpillar
rake
nest
sticks
grass
pram
vegetables
bonfire
hosepipe
greenhouse

The workshop

vice

screws

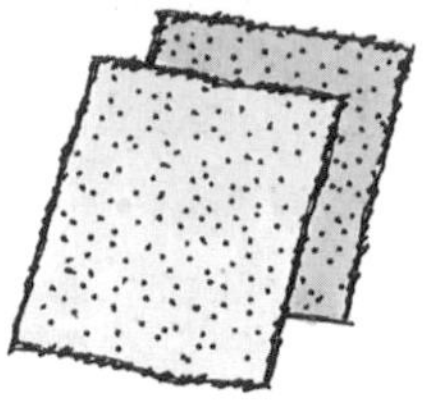
sandpaper

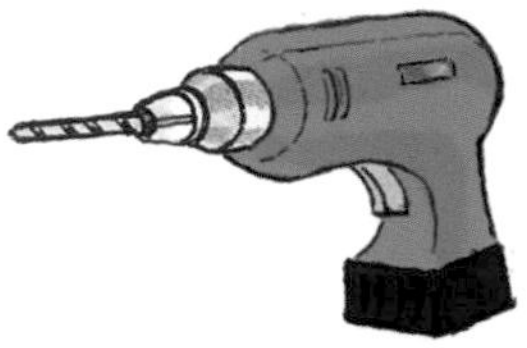
drill

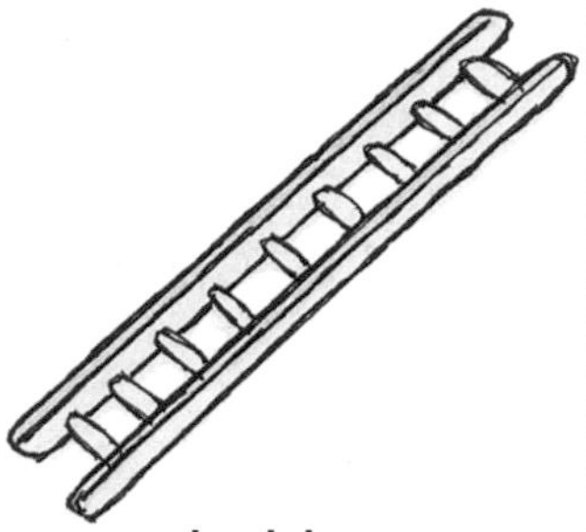
ladder

saw

sawdust

calendar

toolbox

screwdriver

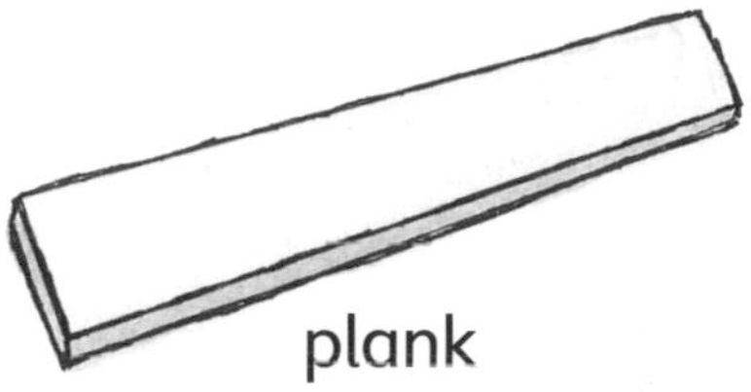
plank

shavings

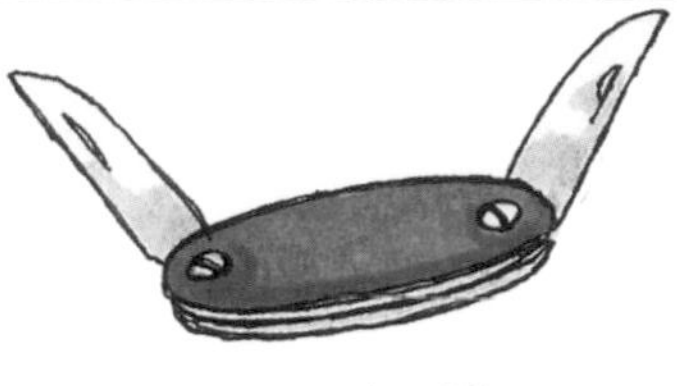
penknife

tacks
spider
bolts
nuts
cobweb
barrel
fly
axe
tape measure
hammer
file
paint pot
plane
wood
nails
workbench
jars

The street

shop

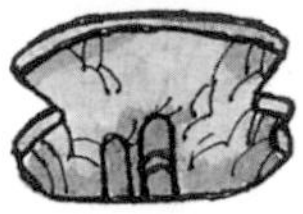

hole

café

ambulance

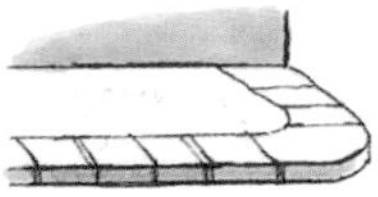

pavement

statue

chimney

roof

digger

hotel

bus

man

police car

pipes

drill

school

playground

taxi
crossing
factory
lorry
traffic lights
cinema
van
roller
trailer
house
market
steps
motorbike
bicycle
fire engine
policeman
car
woman
lamp post
flats

The toyshop

train set

mouth organ

dice

recorder

robot

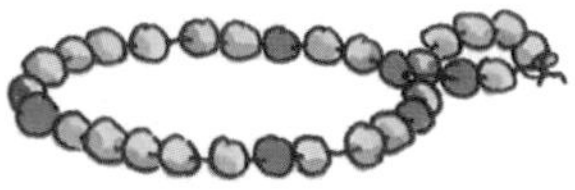
necklace

camera

beads

dolls

guitar

ring

doll's house

whistle

bricks

castle

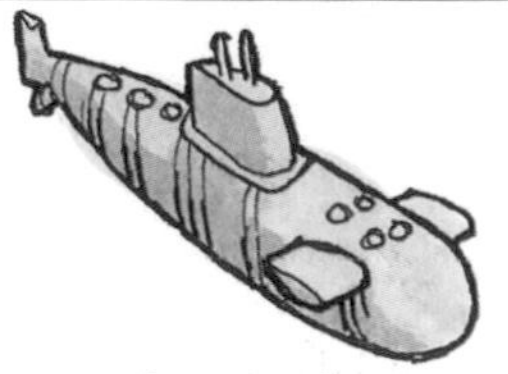
submarine

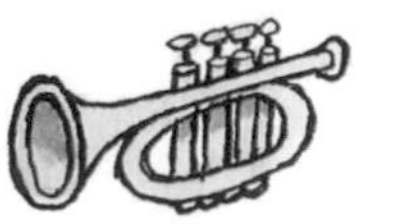
trumpet

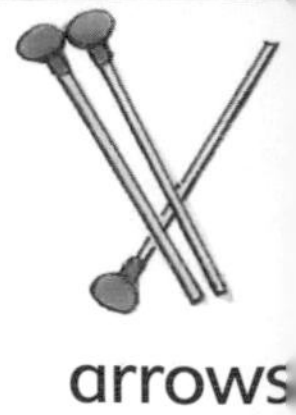
arrows

bow
parachute
boat
face paints
roller
masks
racing car
rocking horse
money box
marbles
puppets
piano
spacemen
crane
playing cards
drums
soldiers
paints
rocket

The park

swings

bench

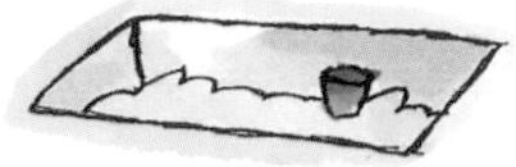
sandpit

picnic

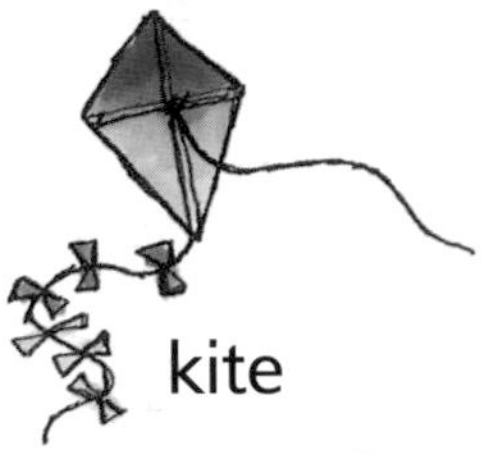
kite

ice cream

dog

gate

path

frog

slide

tadpoles

lake

roller blades

bush

baby
skateboard
earth
pushchair
seesaw
children
tricycle
birds
railings
ball
yacht
string
puddle
ducklings
skipping rope
flower bed
swans
lead
ducks
trees

Animals

hippopotamus

wing
eagle
panda
gorilla
paws
kangaroo
bat
monkey
tail
wolf
iceberg
penguin
crocodile
bear
feathers
pelican
ostrich
dolphin
giraffe
lion
cubs

deer
camel
seal
polar bear
tortoise
elephant
trunk
rhinoceros
bison
zebra
beaver
horns
goat
shark
snake
whale
tiger
leopard

Travel

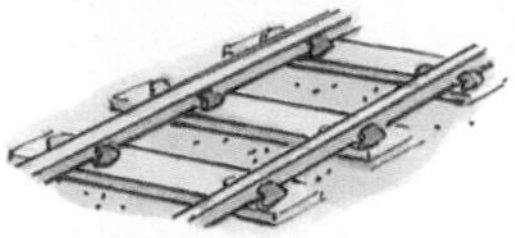
railway track

engine

buffers

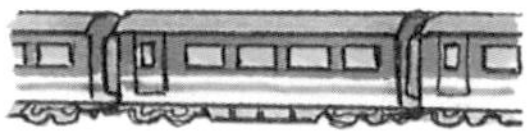
carriages

train driver

goods train

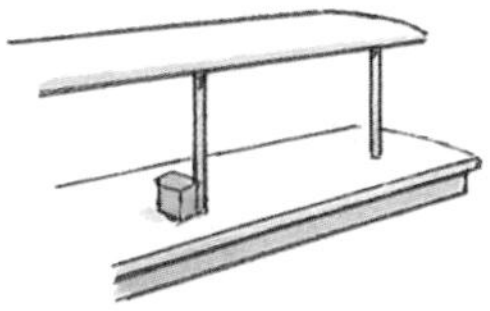
platform

ticket inspector

suitcase

ticket machine

The railway station

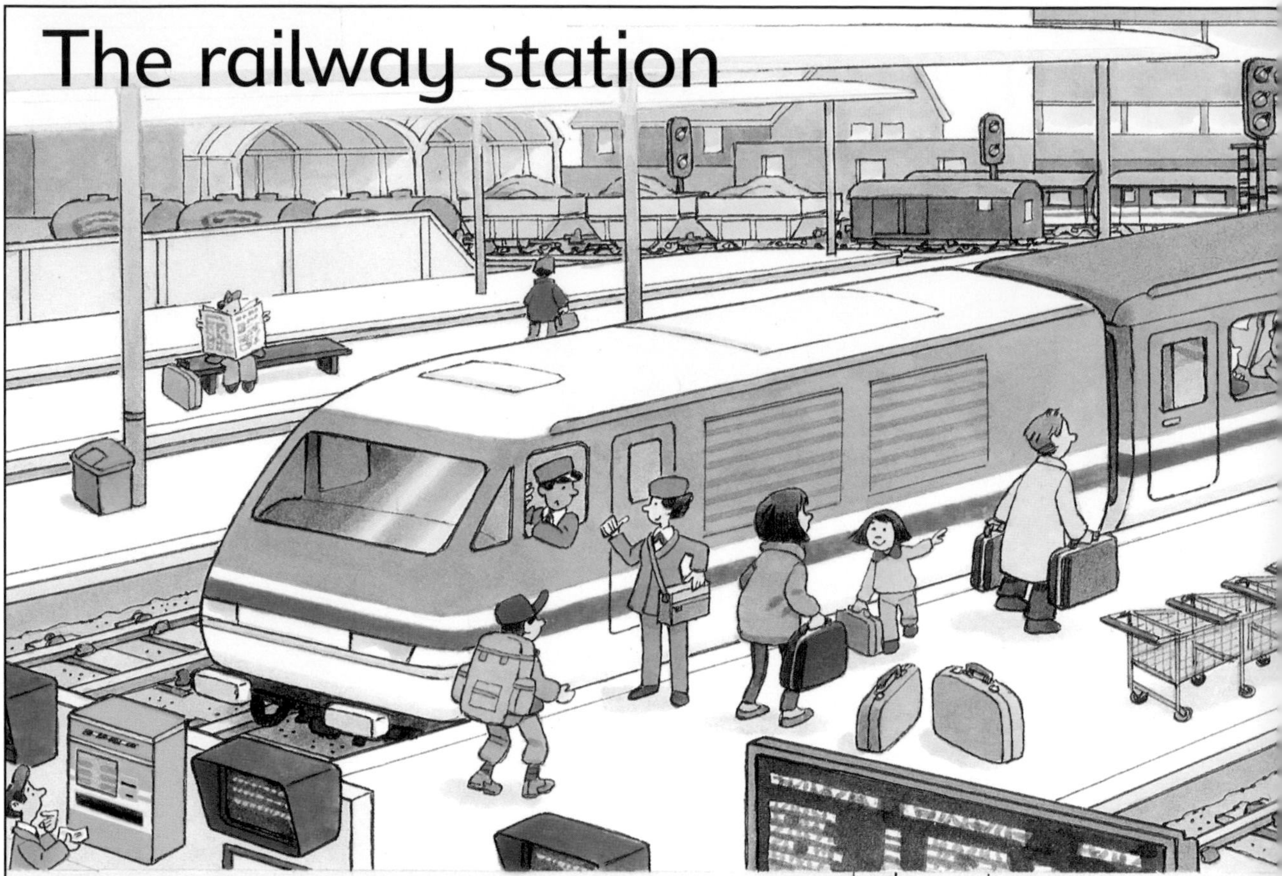

The garage

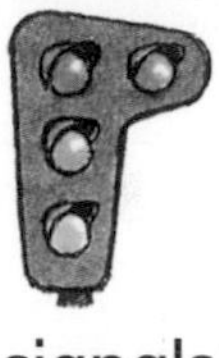
signals

backpack

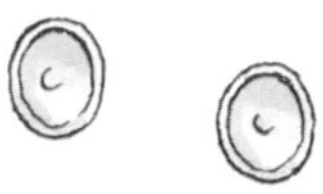
headlights

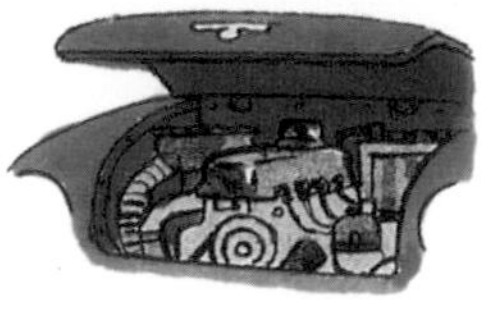
engine

wheel

battery

plane

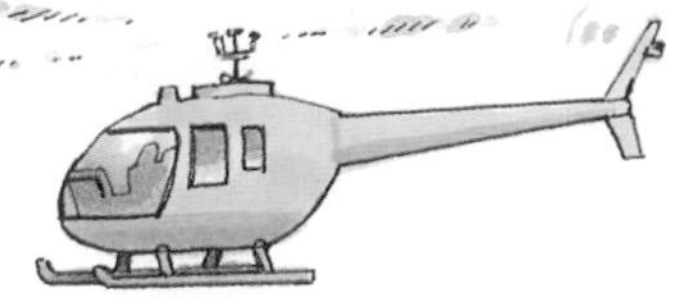
helicopter

runway

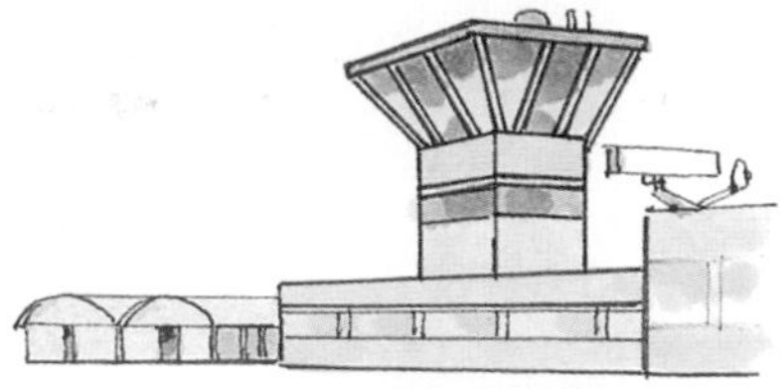
control tower

The airport

car wash

cabin crew

pilot

car wash

boot

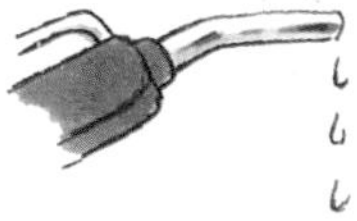
petrol

breakdown lorry

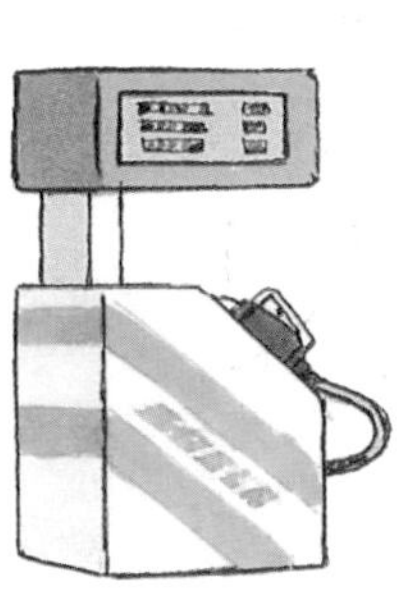
petrol pump

petrol tanker

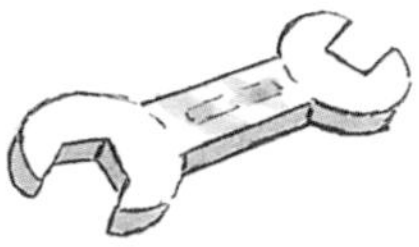
spanner

tyre

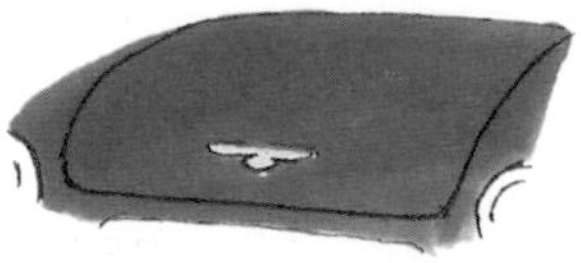
bonnet

oil

The country

windmill

mountain

hot-air balloon

butterfly

lizard

stones

fox

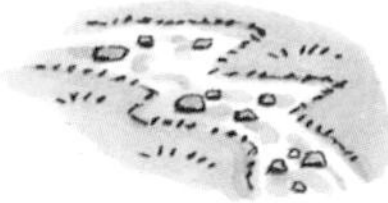
stream

signpost

hedgehog

lock

squirrel

forest

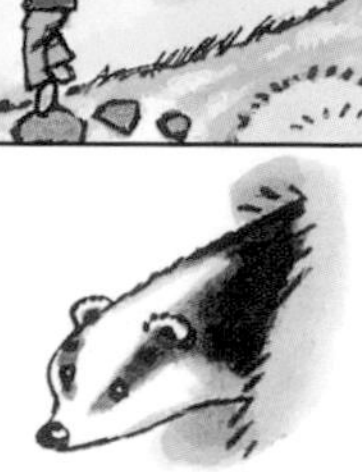
badger

river

road

tents
canal
logs
village
moth
bridge
barge
waterfall
owl
tunnel
fox cubs
mole
fisherman
rocks
toad
train
caravan
hill

The farm

haystack

cockerel

sheepdog

lambs

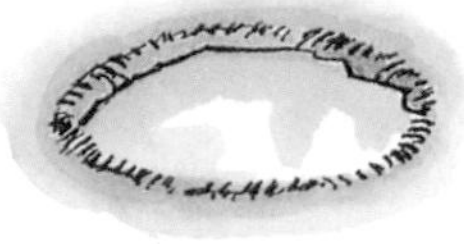
pond

chicks

hayloft

pigsty

bull

hen house

tractor

geese

tanker

barn

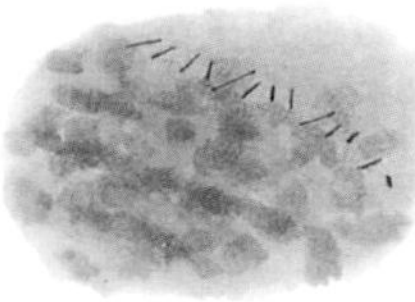
mud

cart

farmer

field

hens

calf

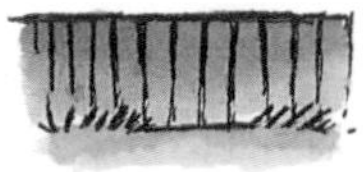
fence

saddle

cowshed

cow

plough

orchard

stable

piglets

donkey

turkeys

scarecrow

hay

sheep

straw bales

horse

pigs

farmhouse

The seaside

sailing boat

shell

sea

oar

lighthouse

spade

bucket

starfish

sandcastle

umbrella

flag

sailor

crab

seagull

island

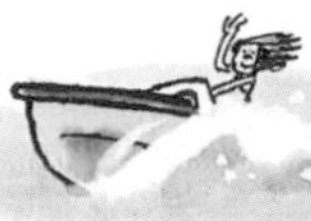

motorboat

water-skier

waves
sunhat
cliff
ship
canoe
rope
pebbles
seaweed
net
paddle
fishing boat
flippers
suncream
fish
swimsuit
oil tanker
beach
rowing boat
deckchair

At school

scissors

2 + 2 = 4
2 + 3 = 5

sums

board

rubber

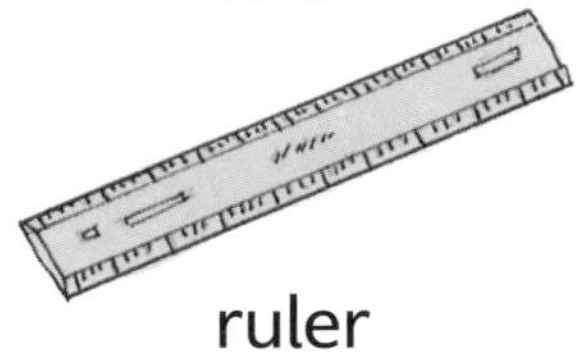

ruler

photographs

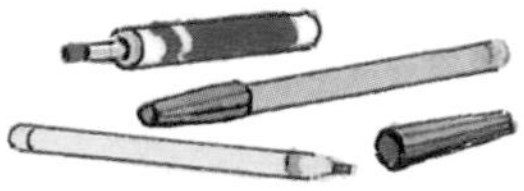

felt-tips

clay

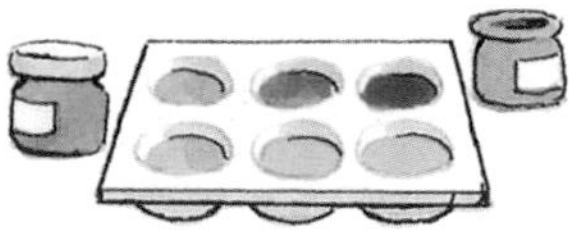

paints

boy

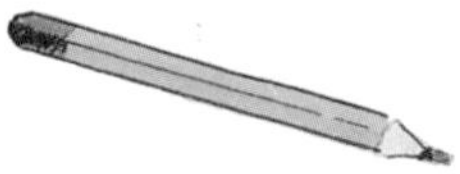

pencil

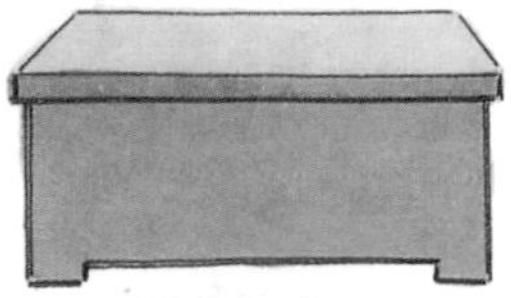

desk

books

pen

glue

chalk

drawing

wastepaper bin

teacher

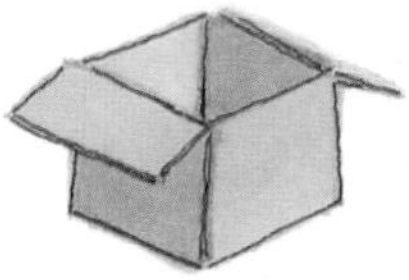
box

map

brush

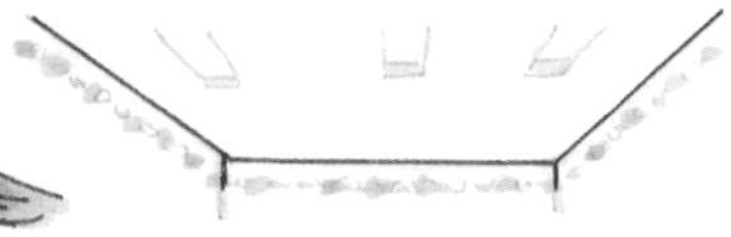
ceiling

a b c d e f
g h i j k l m
n o p q r s t
u v w x y z
2+2=4
2+3=5

wall

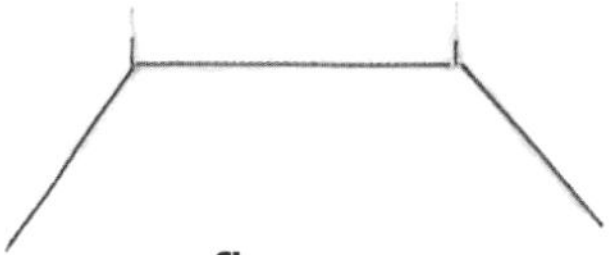
floor

notebook

a b c d e f
g h i j k l m
n o p q r s t
u v w x y z

alphabet

badge

aquarium

paper

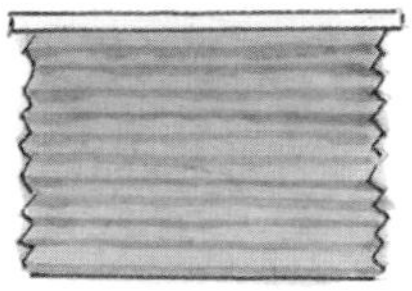
blind

easel

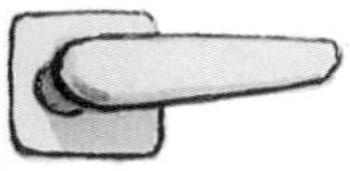
door handle

plant

globe

girl

crayons

lamp

The hospital

apple

nurse

cotton wool

medicine

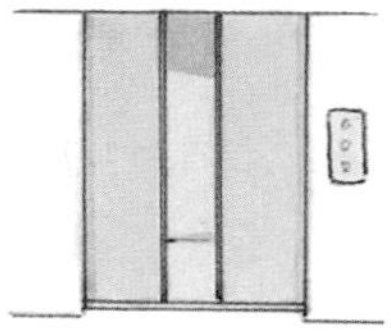
lift

dressing gown

crutches

pills

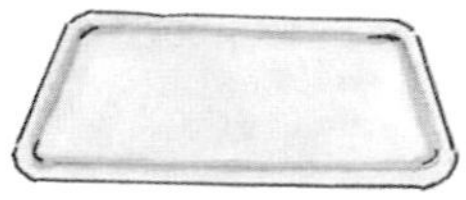
tray

watch

thermometer

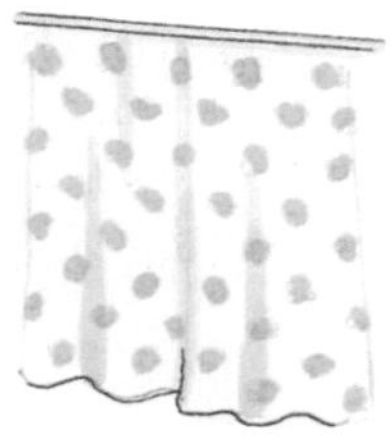
curtain

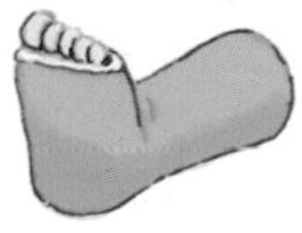
cast

bandage

wheelchair

jigsaw

doctor

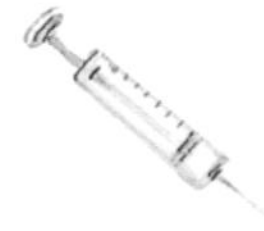
syringe

The doctor

slippers

computer

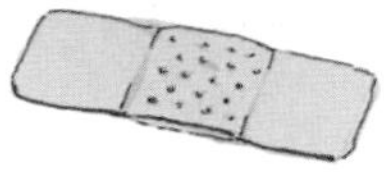
sticking plaster

banana

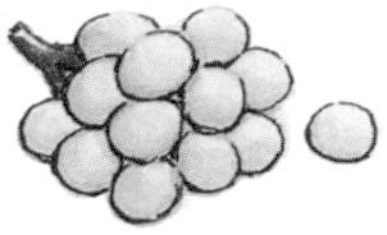
grapes

basket

toys

pear

cards

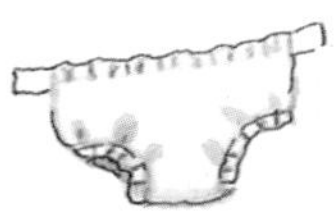
nappy

walking stick

pillow

nightdress

pyjamas

orange

tissues

comic

waiting room

The party

presents

balloon

chocolate

glasses

sweet

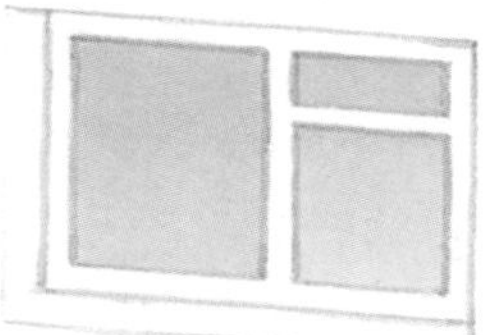

window

fireworks

ribbon

cake

straw

candle

paper chains

toys

clementine

salami

teddy bear

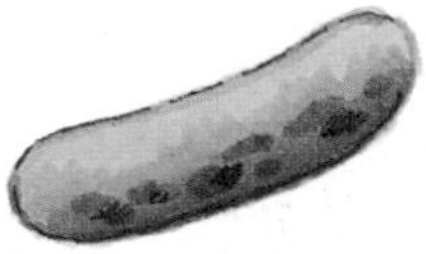
sausage

crisps

fancy dress

cherry

fruit juice

raspberry

strawberry

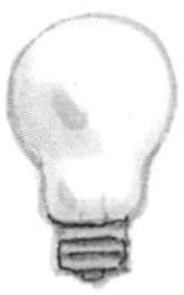
lightbulb

sandwich

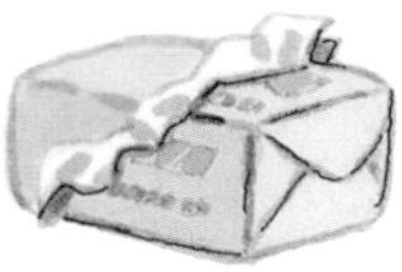
butter

biscuit

cheese

bread

tablecloth

The shop

grapefruit

carrot

cauliflower

leek

mushroom

cucumber

lemon

celery

apricot

melon

carrier bag

CHEESE
FRUIT AND VEGETABLES

onion

cabbage

peach

lettuce

peas

tomato

eggs

plum

flour

scales

jars

meat

pineapple

yoghurt

basket

bottles

handbag

purse

money

tins

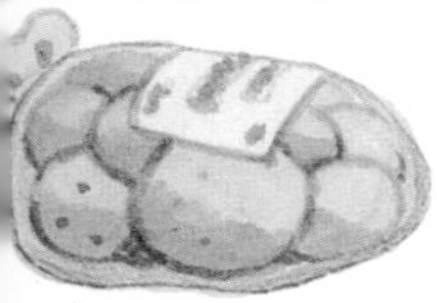
potatoes

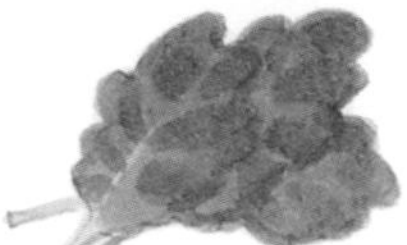
spinach

beans

checkout

pumpkin

trolley

Food

lunch or dinner

breakfast

boiled egg

coffee

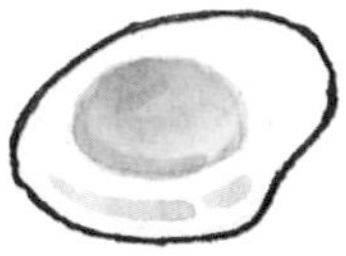

fried egg

toast

jam

cream

milk

cereal

hot chocolate

honey

sugar

salt

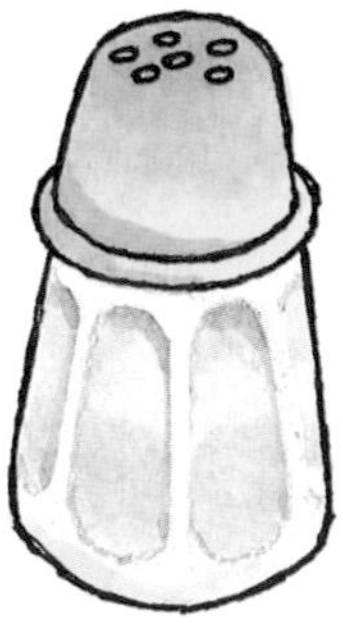

pepper

tea

teapot

pancakes

rolls

supper or dinner

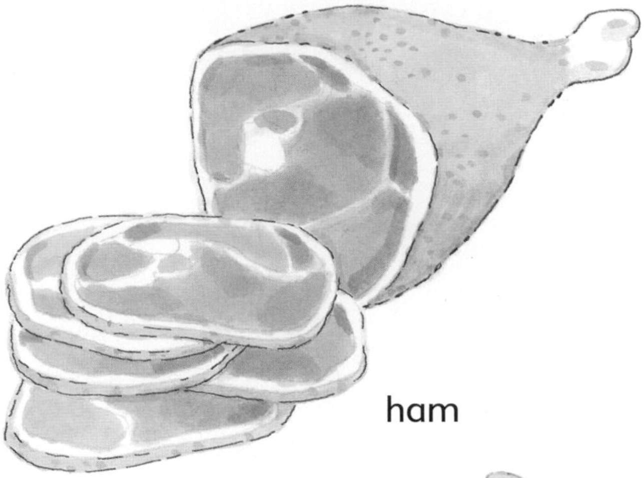

ham

soup

omelette

salad

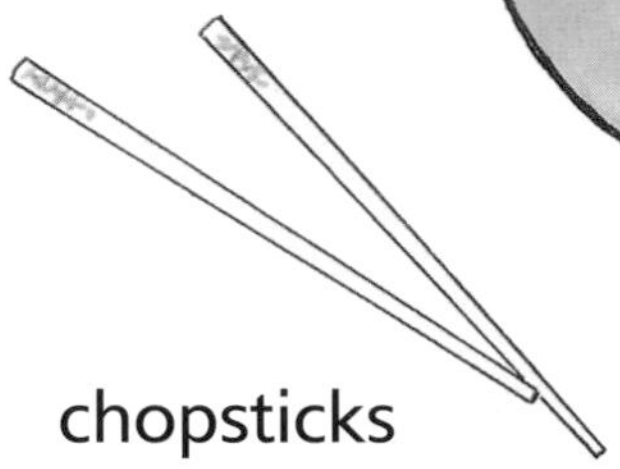

chopsticks

hamburger

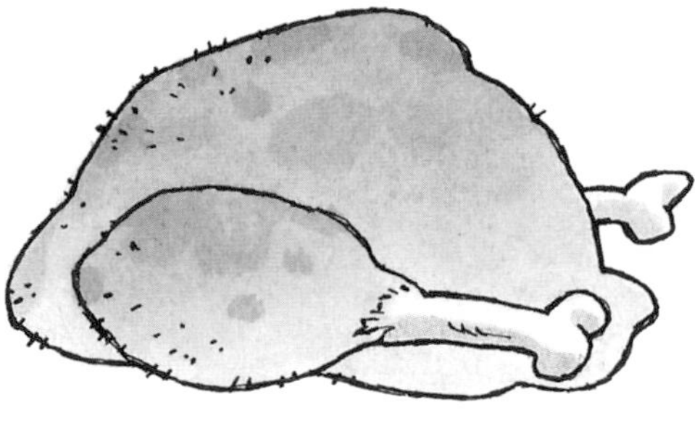

chicken

rice

sauce

spaghetti

mashed potatoes

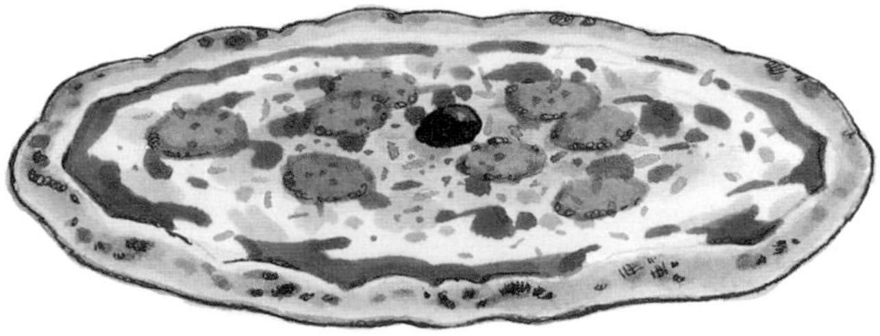

pizza

chips

pudding

Me

head
hair
face

eyebrow

eye

nose

cheek

mouth

lips

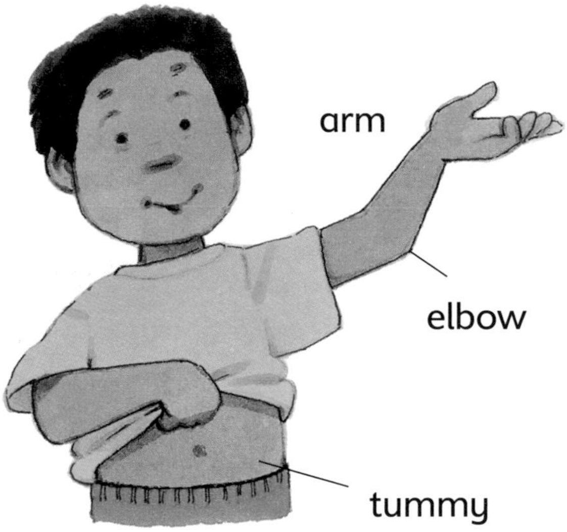
arm
elbow
tummy

teeth

tongue

chin

ears

neck

shoulders

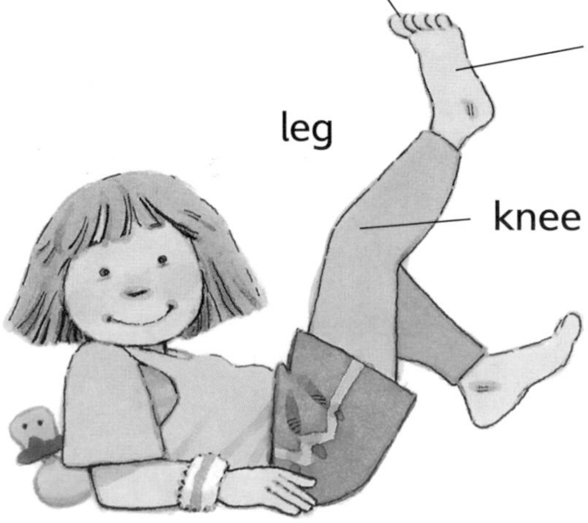
toes
foot
leg
knee

chest

back

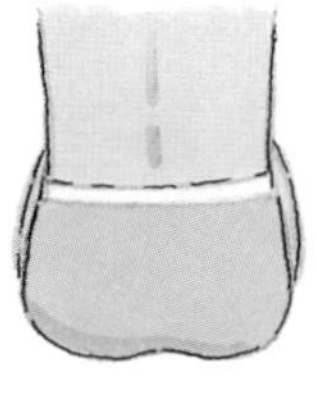
bottom

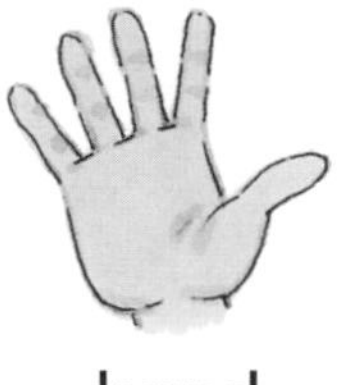
hand

thumb

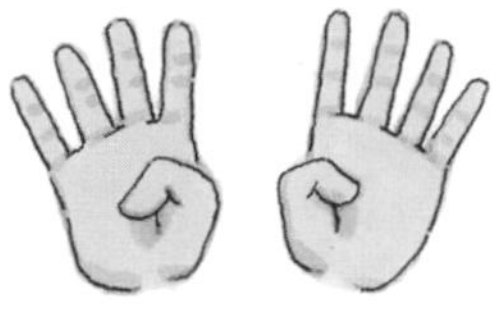
fingers

My clothes

socks

pants

vest

trousers

jeans

T-shirt

skirt

shirt

tie

shorts

tights

dress

jumper

sweatshirt

cardigan

scarf

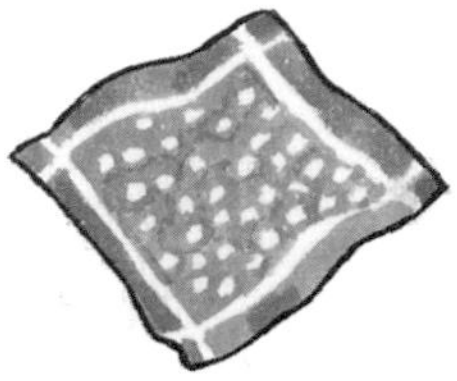
handkerchief

trainers

shoes

sandals

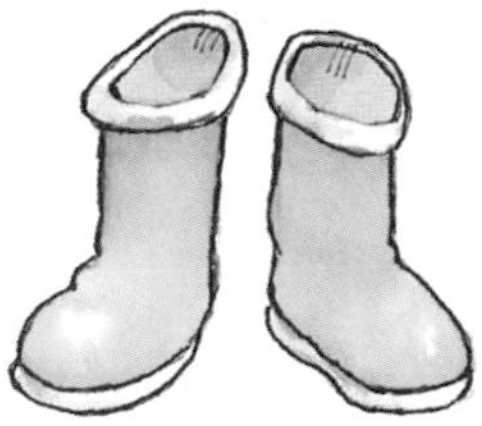
boots

gloves

belt

buckle

zip

shoelace

buttons

button holes

pockets

coat

jacket

cap

hat

People

actor actress

chef

dancers

singers

astronaut

butcher

policeman

policewoman

carpenter

firefighter

artist

judge

mechanics

hairdresser

lorry driver

bus driver

waiter   waitress

postman

dentist

diver

painter

baker

Families

son
brother

daughter
sister

mother
wife

father
husband

aunt

uncle

pet

cousin

grandfather

grandmother

Doing things

laugh

smile
cry
think
listen
catch
throw
break
paint
write
chop
cut
eat
talk
dig
carry
drink
make
jump
crawl
dance
wash
knit

play

watch

climb

take

skip

sleep

fight

sew

wait

hide

cook

read

buy

push

sing

pull

blow

sweep

pick

fall

walk

run

sit

Opposite words

far
near
good
bad
cold
hot
wet
dry
top
bottom
dirty
clean
over
under
fat
thin
open
closed
small
big
few
many
first
last
left

out

in

easy

difficult

empty

full

soft

hard

front

high

slow

fast

back

low

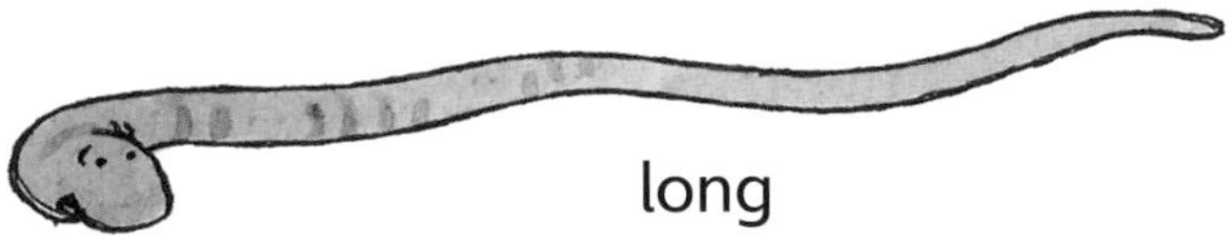
long

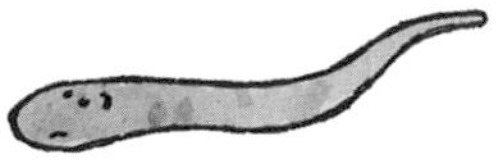
short

dead

alive

dark

light

old

upstairs

downstairs

right

new

Days

Monday
Tuesday
Wednesday
Thursday
Friday
Saturday
Sunday
calendar

morning

evening

sun

night

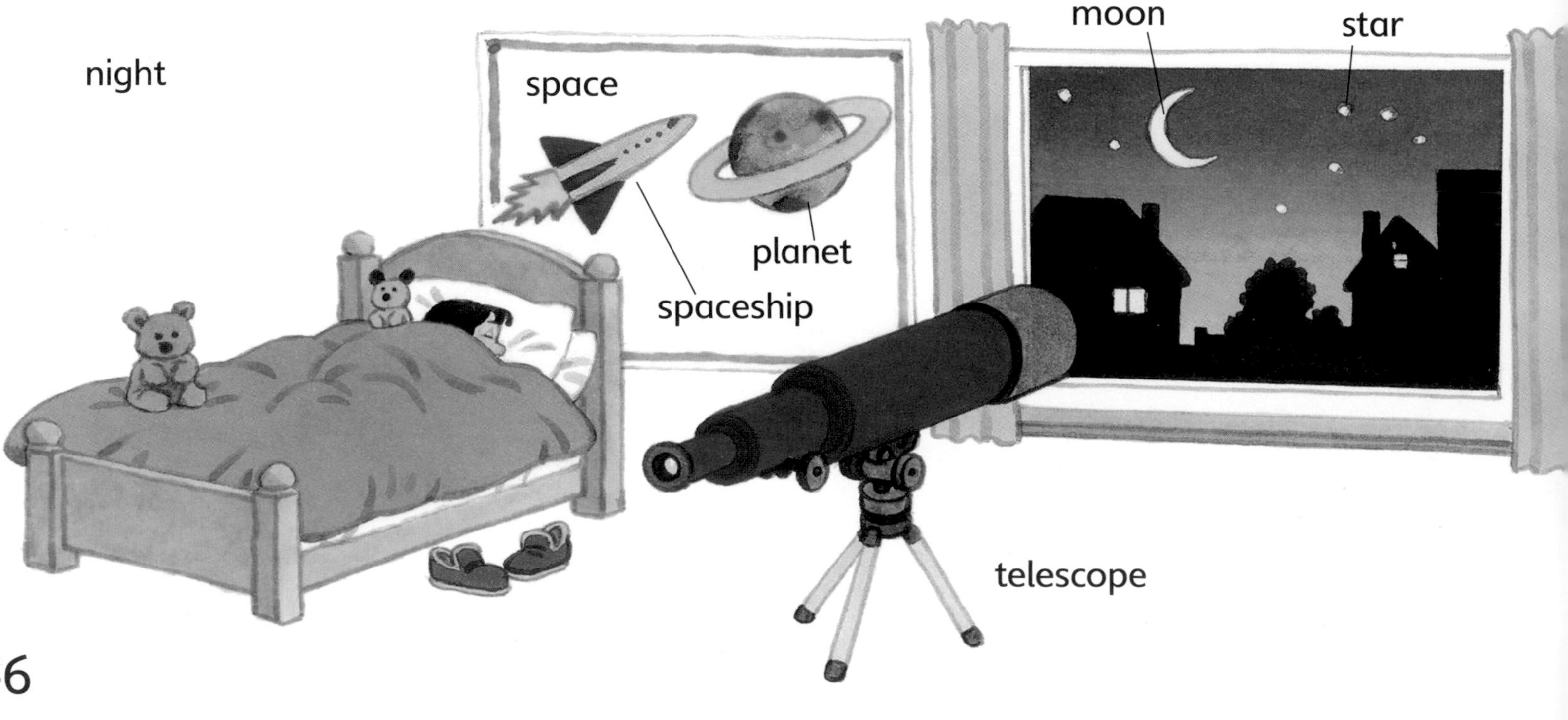
space
spaceship
planet
moon
star
telescope

Special days

birthday
birthday card
candle
present
birthday cake

holiday

wedding day
guests
bridesmaid
bride
bridegroom

camera
photographer

Christmas day
reindeer
sleigh
Father Christmas
Christmas tree

Weather

sun
clouds
sky

umbrella

rain

lightning

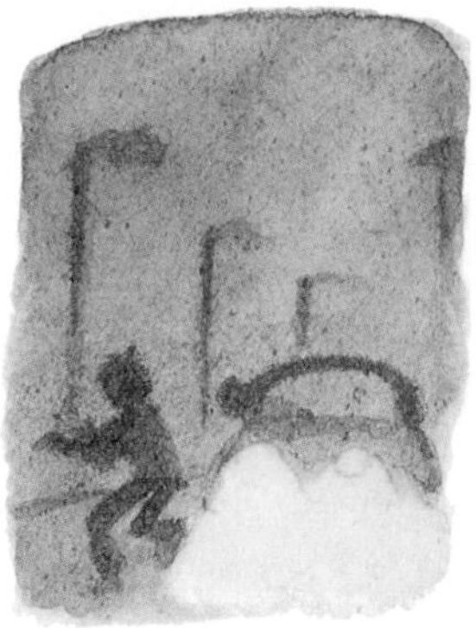

fog

snow

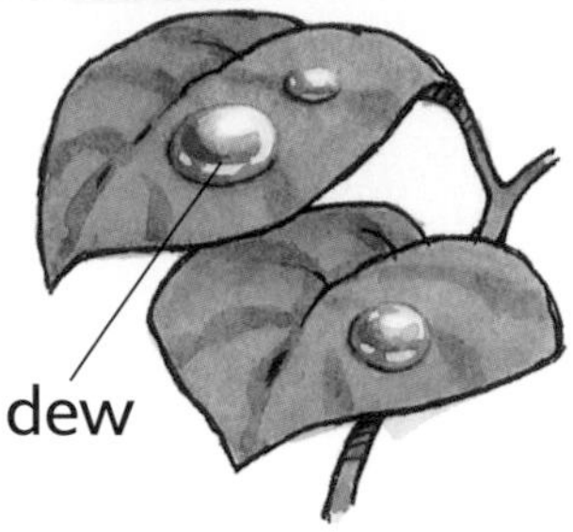
dew

wind

mist

frost

rainbow

Seasons

spring

summer

autumn

winter

Pets

vet

hamster
kennel
guinea pig
dog
budgerigar
puppy
food
parrot
beak
canary
cage
rabbit
cat
basket
kitten
mouse
milk
goldfish

Sport and exercise

basketball
rowing
sail
snowboarding
sailing
windsurfing
cricket
karate
racket
tennis
American football
gym
bat
ball
fishing rod
fishing
bait
rugby
dance
baseball
diving
swimming pool
swimming
race

archery
target
hang-gliding
jogging
helmet
judo
cycling
climbing
locker
horse
pony
football
changing room
riding
badminton
table tennis
ice skates
ice-skating
ski pole
chairlift
ski
skiing
sumo wrestling

Colours

orange
green
black
grey
red
brown
pink
white
blue
purple
yellow

Shapes

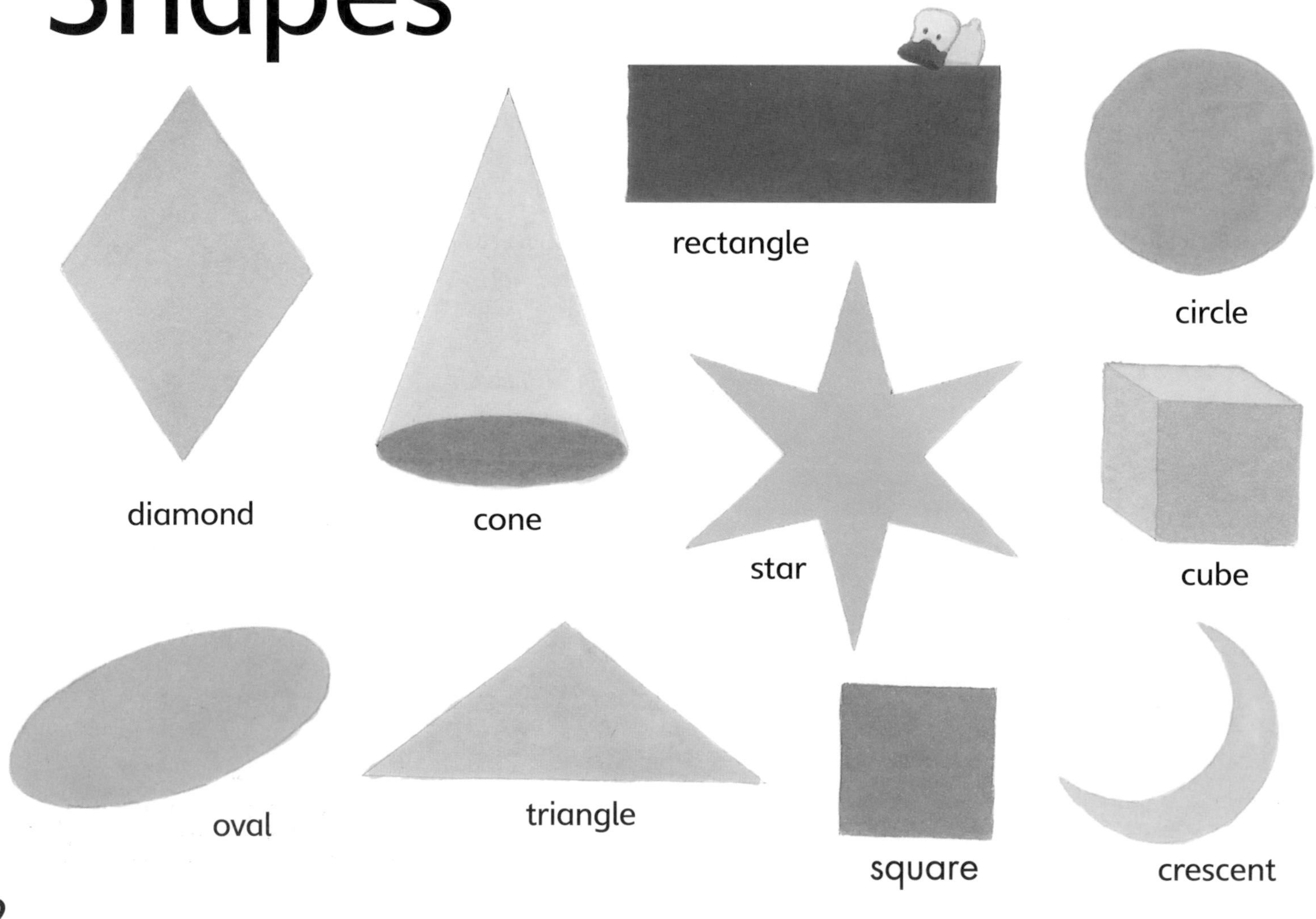
rectangle
circle
diamond
cone
star
cube
oval
triangle
square
crescent

Numbers

1 one
2 two
3 three
4 four
5 five
6 six
7 seven
8 eight
9 nine
10 ten
11 eleven
12 twelve
13 thirteen
14 fourteen
15 fifteen
16 sixteen
17 seventeen
18 eighteen
19 nineteen
20 twenty

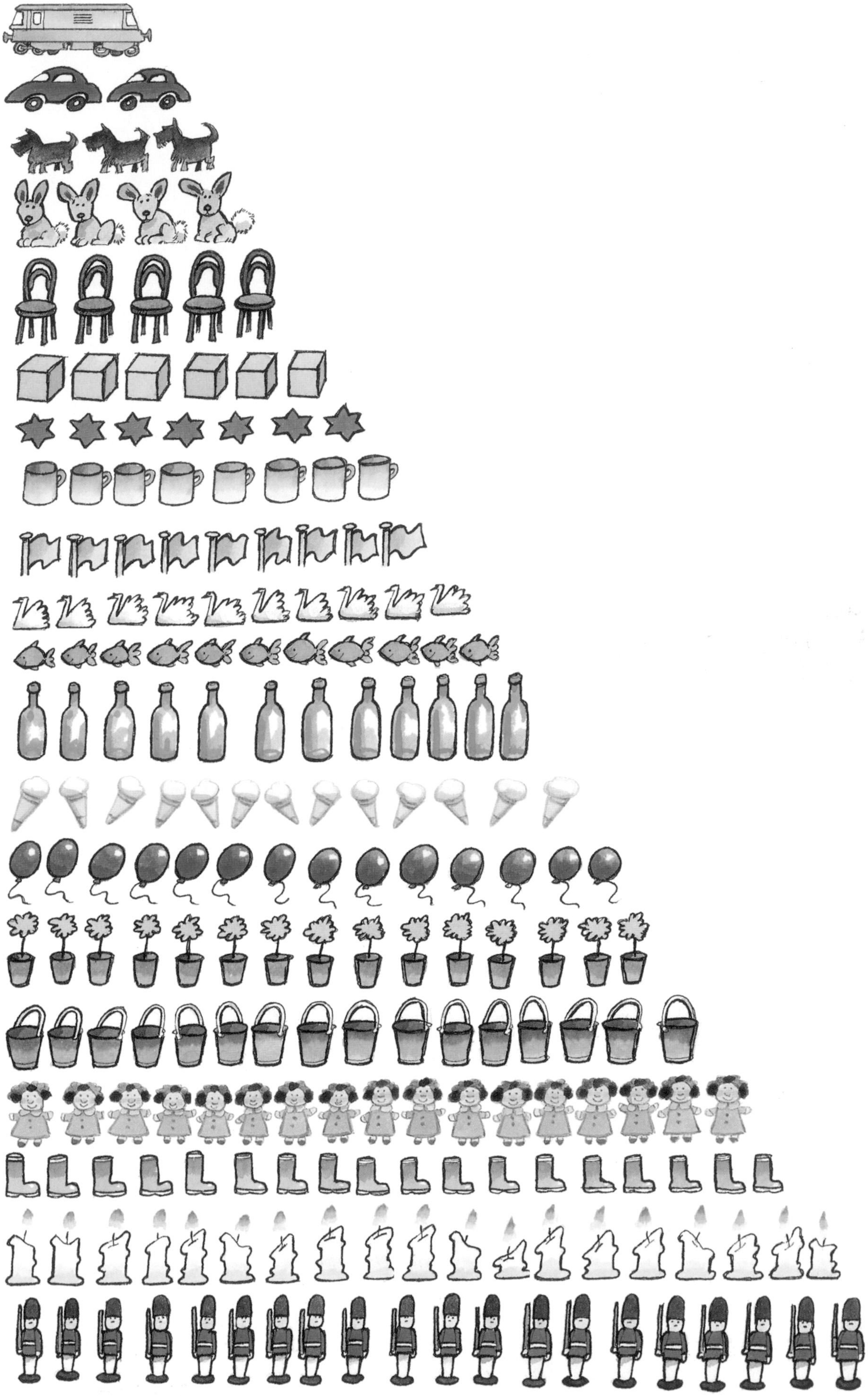

The fairground

big wheel

roundabout

candy floss

ghost train

popcorn

helter-skelter

mat

dodgems

hoop-la

rollercoaster

The circus

trapeze
tightrope walker
pole
tightrope
rope ladder
safety net
trick cyclist
acrobats
juggler
rabbit
ringmaster
dog
hoop
top hat
bow tie
band
bareback rider
clown

Words in order

This is a list of all the words in the pictures, in alphabetical order. After each word is a page number. On that page, you will find the word and picture together.

a

b

e

f

g

r

s

t

u

v

w

y

z